C000108692

IMAGES
of Sport

WARRINGTON
RUGBY LEAGUE CLUB
1970-2000

Captain fantastic. Skipper Ken Kelly holds aloft the John Player Trophy after leading Warrington to a 12-5 victory over Barrow. The final, in January 1981, attracted a (then) record crowd of 12,820 to Central Park, Wigan. Following closely behind Kelly is full-back Steve Hesford who kicked two goals and two drop goals in the final. Both players would go on to make more than 300 appearances for the Wire.

IMAGES
of Sport

WARRINGTON
RUGBY LEAGUE CLUB
1970-2000

Compiled by
Eddie Fuller and Gary Slater

TEMPUS

First published 2000
Copyright © Eddie Fuller and Gary Slater, 2000

Tempus Publishing Limited
The Mill, Brimscombe Port,
Stroud, Gloucestershire, GL5 2QG

ISBN 0 7524 1870 X

Typesetting and origination by
Tempus Publishing Limited
Printed in Great Britain by
Midway Clark Printing, Wiltshire

This book is dedicated to all the supporters, directors and officials who have stuck by the club, through thick and thin, over the past thirty years – supporters like Stan Lewandowski, Craig Garner and Ernie Day; directors like Phil Worthington, Clarrie Owen and Bill Garratt and officials like Ron Close and John Smith. We hope you enjoy the book.

Top man. Warrington captain Les Boyd with the Premiership Trophy and the Harry Sunderland Man of the Match award after the 38-10 victory over Halifax at Elland Road, Leeds in May 1986.

Contents

Memories   6

Foreword   7

Introduction   9

1.   The Arrival of Ossie Davies and Alex Murphy: The 1970s   11

2.   The Australian Invasion: The 1980s   53

3.   The Dawn of Super League: The 1990s   99

Flying machine. Prop-forward Dave Chisnall dives in for one of the 24 tries he scored for Warrington during his first spell at Wilderspool.

Memories

Thirty seasons in the history of Warrington Rugby League Club and magical moments flash through the mind faster than film through a motor wind.

Although my first camera at Wilderspool featured no such action-assisted device, the single-shot photographic images it recorded made even darkroom developing a fascinating experience. The year was 1972 and I was recording, for the first time, the power and spectacle of Rugby League in print. After many years of covering sport, mostly football, the raw courage of Dave Chisnall, Kevin Ashcroft and Brian Brady taking on opposition front rows of equal bravery made soccer look to me like a game for girls!

Their efforts, coupled with feats of spectacular try scoring and the inspirational leadership of Alex Murphy, made my task less of a job than a passion. Great players and moments in the years since then have been too many to mention and it was difficult to select which players and incidents should be featured in this book.

Some 192 photographs have been included from more than 3,000 that have been published in the *Warrington Guardian* and the club programme. Each one brings the memories flooding back.

Eddie Fuller
February 2000

All smiles. Warrington Wolves chief executive Peter Deakin (left) with coach Darryl Van de Velde (right) and chairman Lord Hoyle.

Foreword

Here at Wilderspool we are planning for an exciting future, but we have not forgotten the heroic deeds of the past and, in particular, the last thirty years.

For the start of Super League V we have signed giant Australian prop Andrew Gee from Brisbane Broncos in the belief that he will carry on the tradition of dynamic forward play associated with players like Les Boyd and Dave Chisnall.

We have also secured the services of legendary Australian scrum-half Allan 'Alfie' Langer and are confident that he will prove a worthy successor to men like Ken Kelly and Parry Gordon. We have also captured Tawera Nikau from Australian champions Melbourne Storm, convinced that he will follow in the giant footsteps of this club's exceptional loose-forwards, like Barry Philbin and Mike Gregory.

Planning for the future, yet remembering the past; Eddie Fuller and Gary Slater are both outstanding journalists and dedicated Warrington fans. They share my hopes for the future and my respect for the past and so I am honoured to support this pictorial history.

Peter Deakin
Chief Executive
Warrington Wolves Rugby League Club

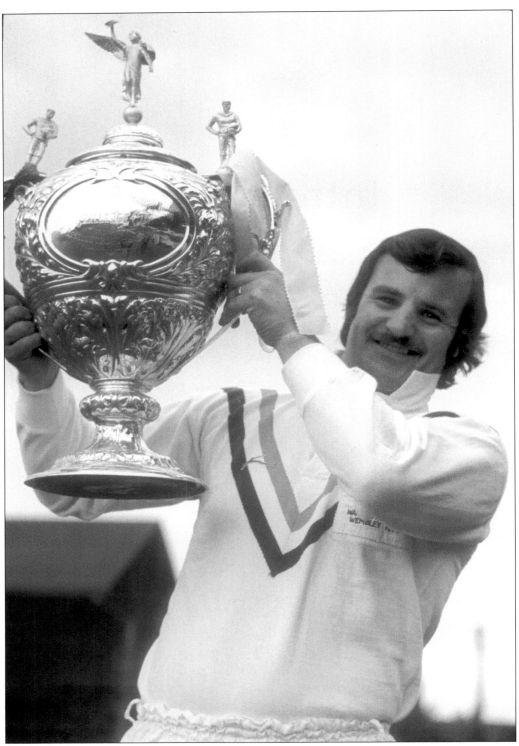

Alex Murphy with the Challenge Cup, 1974 (see pp. 21-25).

Introduction

The 1970/71 season was Warrington's worst – on and off the pitch. It started with a record five defeats in a row and showed few signs of improvement. Coach Joe Egan resigned in September and was replaced by former player Peter Harvey, the 'A' team coach, but the underlying problem remained. Warrington were £33,000 in debt – a huge sum. At the end of October, W.L. Challinor, the club chairman, launched a public appeal for funds. Unless £10,000 was raised by the end of the season, the club would close.

Warrington needed a knight in shining armour. Fortunately, one arrived in the form of Mr Oswald 'Ossie' Davies who bought a controlling interest in the club in May 1971. His first major decision as chairman was to appoint the legendary Alex Murphy as player-coach just five days after Murphy had led Leigh to a stunning 24-7 Challenge Cup final victory over red-hot favourites Leeds at Wembley. It was an inspired move and six major trophies followed in the next seven seasons. During the 1973/74 season alone, the Wire lifted four cups and were rightly hailed as the best team in the country.

Success, however, came at a price and by 1976 Warrington were again experiencing financial problems. On this occasion a group of dedicated supporters decided to do something to help and in August 1976 the Primrose Association was formed to raise funds to buy players. Over the next few seasons thousands of pounds were raised through a variety of social functions and, by and large, the money was spent wisely. The most significant signing using the Primrose Association cash was that of former St Helens scrum-half Ken Kelly, from Bradford Northern, for £6,000.

Kelly joined Warrington on loan in December 1976 but, at Wigan in only his fourth match for the Wire, he suffered a broken arm. Warrington completed the transfer while he was still injured and what a signing he proved to be. Over the next ten years, he made 301 appearances, scoring 73 tries, and becoming one of the most successful captains in the club's history, guiding Warrington to success in the Lancashire Cup in 1980 and again in 1982. He also led the Wire to victory in the 1981 John Player Trophy final during another season when the team could claim to be the best in the business.

Another fallow period followed until Peter Higham took over as chairman in 1984. One of his first initiatives was to launch a major fund-raising effort called the Lifeline Society whereby supporters paid £1 a week for the chance to win £1,000 a week. Lifeline would prove to be a tremendous success and raise thousands of pounds for the club. At first, the money was needed to pay off debts but soon it was used to fund the signings of top-quality overseas players, like Australian full-back Brian Johnson, New Zealand Test forward Kevin Tamati and fiery Aussie legend Les Boyd.

Boyd, in particular, became a folk hero at Wilderspool and inspired the Wire to victory in the 1986 Premiership final at Elland Road by scoring two of their seven tries in a comprehensive 38-10 triumph. Boyd was offered the post of Warrington coach in November 1988 but could not take it for business reasons. The job instead went to Brian Johnson and for the next seven years he kept the club at the forefront of the British game. In his first full season in charge, with Great Britain loose-forward Mike Gregory leading from the front, Warrington won the Lancashire Cup and reached the Challenge Cup final for the first time in fifteen years.

The following season the Wire lifted the Regal Trophy by beating Bradford Northern 12-2 in the final at Headingley, having already seen off a star-studded Widnes team 8-4 in a thrilling semi-final at Central Park.

The 1993/94 season was another memorable campaign with Warrington transformed into championship challengers by the arrival of Welsh genius Jonathan Davies from Widnes on a free transfer. Widnes were in dire financial straits and could no longer afford to pay Davies' expensive contract, but Davies proved to be worth every penny of his executive salary. At a stroke he provided Warrington with a top-class goalkicker, genuine pace in the centre and star quality.

The Johnson era came to an end with a humiliating 80-0 defeat at St Helens in the semi-finals of the Regal Trophy in January 1996. Warrington turned to the dream team of Alex Murphy and John Dorahy, the former Wigan coach, to revive their flagging fortunes and propel the club into Super League. Murphy proclaimed: 'John Dorahy will come back to haunt Wigan – and that is a promise. John and I reckon we need something like eight class players. It's about time we had craftsmen helping this club's top youngsters instead of the other way round. But we will consider only the best. No money will be wasted on second-raters.'

Fine words, but when Dorahy resigned in March 1997 Warrington were still struggling on the pitch and their debts had reached nightmare proportions. He did not know it at the time but the next Warrington coach, Darryl Van de Velde, was taking on the biggest challenge of his career. In October 1998 a consortium attempting to buy the club collapsed, leaving Warrington on the brink of extinction. Mercifully, Warrington Borough Council stepped in to save the club by agreeing to buy Wilderspool for almost £1million – a figure that was not enough to pay off all the club's debts but one which gave the Wolves a second chance. A takeover of the club was completed in December 1998 and Warrington began to claw their way back to the top.

In January 1999, Warrington stunned Super League by making two major signings. Former St Helens and Great Britain centre Alan Hunte, who was still only twenty-eight, arrived from Hull Sharks and he was quickly followed by a new chief executive, Peter Deakin, the man who had re-marketed Bradford Bulls and the Saracens Rugby Union club. The revival gathered greater impetus in August 1999 when Warrington secured the services of two exceptional Australian players – scrum-half Allan Langer and prop-forward Andrew Gee – ready for the start of Super League V. New Zealand Test loose-forward Tawera Nikau was signed in October and England stand-off Steve Blakeley followed in November. Once again, optimism reigned at Wilderspool.

Gary Slater
December 1999

One
The Arrival of Ossie Davies and Alex Murphy:
The 1970s

Muddy marvel. Warrington captain Parry Gordon holds aloft the John Player Trophy after the surprise victory over arch-rivals Widnes in the mud at Knowsley Road, St Helens, in January 1978. Gordon made an incredible 528 full first-team appearances for the club from his debut in 1963 to his final match in 1981, scoring 167 tries.

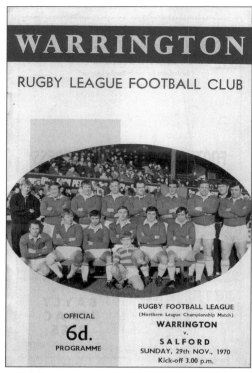

WARRINGTON

RUGBY LEAGUE FOOTBALL CLUB

OFFICIAL
6d.
PROGRAMME

RUGBY FOOTBALL LEAGUE
(Northern League Championship Match)
WARRINGTON
v.
SALFORD
SUNDAY, 29th NOV., 1970
Kick-off 3.00 p.m.

Bloody Sunday. Warrington hit rock bottom on Sunday 29 November 1970, when they were humbled 50-0 by Salford at Wilderspool – a record home defeat. Almost thirty years later the mere mention of the game still brings the painful memories flooding back for Parry Gordon, who was the Warrington scrum-half that day. Full-back Derek Whitehead, another who would go on to achieve great things in the years to follow, missed the match through injury. Warrington were losing 29-0 at half-time and went on to concede twelve tries in total. Jack Steel in the *Warrington Guardian* described it as the 'ultimate in demoralisation' and, not surprisingly perhaps, some supporters forgot the game during the second half and turned their anger at the directors' box. Six days after the Salford debacle, Warrington suffered another crushing loss, 48-8 at Leeds. This was a club in crisis. Warrington fans started voting with their feet and the 1,705 who turned up for the home game against Oldham in December formed Wilderspool's lowest gate since the war.

Soldiering on. Warrington versus Featherstone Rovers, January 1971. From left to right, back row: Conrad Barton, Jackie Brennan, Phil Jones, Joe Doherty, Peter Cannon, Ken Parr, Tony Scahill, Brian Brady. Front row: Parry Gordon, Jackie Melling, Dave Harrison, Ken Halliwell (captain), Tommy Conroy, Bob Fleet, Derek Whitehead. The mascot was Steve Walsh. Warrington won 24-17 with Whitehead kicking six goals.

Try star. Winger Mick Henighan joined Warrington from Salford in January 1971 and went on to score 30 tries in 62 full appearances for the Wire before moving on to Swinton. He was Warrington's leading try scorer in 1970/71 (with 11) and 1971/72 (with 15). Henighan had a powerful 6ft tall and 13st 7lb frame and was switched to the loose-forward position in December 1971. It was as a No. 13 that he played in all six Challenge Cup ties in the spring of 1972. Warrington swept into the semi-finals only to lose to St Helens 10-6 in a replay at Central Park watched by 32,180 fans.

Chairman of the board. Ossie Davies bought £20,000 worth of shares in Warrington in 1971 and became club chairman. His first major decision was to appoint Alex Murphy as player-coach on 20 May. Plans were also unveiled for a £300,000 leisure centre on the Priory Street side of the ground. Warrington would never be the same again.

Coming through. Bricklayer Brian Gregory was a 6ft 1in and 15st second-row forward who joined Warrington from Heinz Rugby Union Club in Wigan in 1969. Over the next five years he made 107 full appearances for the Wire, scoring 23 tries. He was at his best during the 1972/73 season when he scored 15 tries in 36 full appearances and played for Lancashire against Cumberland and Yorkshire.

Wheelbarrow try. Welsh forward Bobby Wanbon wins the race for one of his 12 tries during the 1972/73 campaign. Wanbon was a former Aberavon and Wales Rugby Union forward who joined Warrington from St Helens for a £2,000 transfer fee in September 1971. He proved to be an inspired signing and over the next seven years he made 148 full appearances for the Wire, scoring 22 tries. He played in two Wembley finals and toured Australia and New Zealand with the Wales Rugby League team in the summer of 1975.

Catch me if you can. Warrington centre/stand-off Wilf Briggs avoids the clutches of Wigan forward Bill Ashurst. Briggs cost Warrington £1,200 from Oldham and became a prolific try scorer at Wilderspool, with 48 touchdowns in 100 full appearances.

Angel face. Rugged second-row forward Mike Nicholas joined Warrington from Aberavon in October 1972 to become the fifth former Aberavon man on the books, following in the footsteps of Bobby Wanbon, Frank Reynolds, Dennis Curling and Clive Jones. Nicholas became a legend at Wilderspool. He made 142 full appearances, during which he was sent off a club record 13 times.

League leaders. Warrington finished top of the league in the 1972/73 season with 27 wins and 2 draws from their 34 matches to earn the League Leaders' Rose Bowl, their first trophy for five years. The Wire received the Rose Bowl on Saturday 28 April before the Championship play-off first round game against Wigan, which they won 30-15. Warrington are pictured on their lap of honour before the game. From left to right: Derek Noonan, Tommy Conroy, player-coach Alex Murphy, Dennis Curling, mascot Steve Walsh, Brian Brady, Wilf Briggs, Mike Philbin, Kevin Ashcroft, Frank Reynolds.

Winging in. Welsh winger Dennis Curling crosses for one of his 16 tries during the 1972/73 campaign. Curling signed for Warrington for £5,000 in August 1972 after topping Aberavon's try scoring list the previous season. Curling, from Port Talbot, went on to make 126 full appearances for the Wire, scoring 35 tries.

Dream debut. John Bevan's first game for Warrington, against Castleford at Wilderspool in September 1973, was a remarkable match. Bevan, who was just twenty-two, had already played Rugby Union for Cardiff, Wales, the Barbarians and the British Lions and scored one of the four Warrington tries in front of 8,253 delighted fans. Warrington won 22-5 but the match also saw prop-forward Joe Price and player-coach Alex Murphy sent off and referee Fred Lindop needed a police escort at the end. Price was subsequently found not guilty by the Rugby Football League disciplinary committee but Murphy was banned for four matches. Bevan recalls, 'Scoring in my first game was a big relief. I still remember the game very well. Alex Murphy got sent off and one of the Castleford lads tried to break my ribs but we beat them by a good margin and there was a good crowd there.'

Marked man. Alex Murphy collected a serious jaw injury at Leeds in the semi-finals of the Captain Morgan Trophy in December 1973. Murphy was then thirty-four and the injury would have finished the playing careers of lesser men but he was driven by the desire to play at Wembley again and would battle back to fitness. The semi-final, which Warrington won 20-13, also marked the debuts of Australian Dave Wright and Warringtonian Ian Mather in the Wire pack.

The Rugby Football League

Captain Morgan Trophy

Final Tie

FEATHERSTONE ROVERS V WARRINGTON

at The Willows, Salford.

Saturday, Jan 26, 1974 Kick-off 2·30 pm.

Official Programme 10p

Celebration time. Warrington celebrate the 4-0 victory over Featherstone Rovers in the Captain Morgan Trophy final at Salford in January 1974. From left to right, standing: Ossie Davies (chairman), Kevin Ashcroft, Derek 'Nobby' Clarke (physiotherapist), Dave Chisnall, Brian Pitchford (director), Tommy Lomax (kit man), Jackie Hamblett (groundsman), Bobby Wanbon, Ian Mather. Front: Derek Whitehead, John Bevan. The final itself was a dour, defensive affair on a cold and wet afternoon. Warrington won thanks to two penalty goals from Whitehead. Both were kicked from 45 yards and earned him the Man of the Match award. The full Warrington team was: Whitehead; M. Philbin, Noonan, Reynolds, Bevan; Whittle, Gordon; Chisnall, Ashcroft, Brady, Wanbon, D. Wright, Mather. Substitutes: Pickup, Price.

Mud larks. Scrum-half Parry Gordon (left) and captain Kevin Ashcroft rejoice after Warrington's 27-16 victory over Rochdale Hornets in the Player's No. 6 Trophy final at Central Park in February 1974. Warrington won by five tries to four after an open and entertaining match with hooker Ashcroft collecting the Man of the Match award after winning the scrum battle 15-5 to supply his team-mates with plenty of possession. Famously, Ashcroft gave his £25 prize to the Wigan groundsman as a tribute to the hard work he had done on the pitch after a morning downpour. Derek Noonan (two), Mike Nicholas, Derek Whitehead and John Bevan scored the Warrington tries with Whitehead also kicking six goals.

Player's Nº6 Trophy Final

PLAYER'S Nº6 | RUGBY LEAGUE 1973-74

CENTRAL PARK, WIGAN,
FEB 9th 1974 KICK OFF 3pm

ROCHDALE HORNETS
v
WARRINGTON

OFFICIAL PROGRAMME   PRICE 10p

Charge! Warrington second-row forward Mike Nicholas splits open the Dewsbury defence during the Challenge Cup semi-final at Central Park in March 1974. Warrington won 17-7 to book a return trip to Wembley after a twenty-year gap.

Try time. Stand-off Alan Whittle steps through the Dewsbury defence for one of the three Warrington tries in the semi-final. Frank Reynolds and John Bevan scored the others. In the background are Warrington forwards Bobby Wanbon (left) and Barry Philbin.

Record makers. By now Warrington were so successful that they released a single *Primrose and Blue* with vocals by the Wire Choir (Warrington Rugby League team and supporters) and music from an electronic organ. The song begins 'Primrose and Blue/For me and for you/They're the colours we all love to see' and continues in a similar vein. Sales figures are not available.

1974 Primrose & Blue

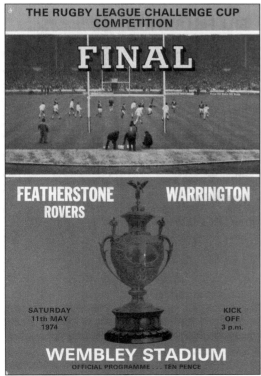

Alex Murphy was listed only as a substitute in the 1974 Challenge Cup final programme but duly lined up as the Warrington stand-off with Alan Whittle moving into the centre. The full Warrington team was: Derek Whitehead; Mike Philbin, Derek Noonan, Alan Whittle, John Bevan; Alex Murphy, Parry Gordon; Dave Chisnall, Kevin Ashcroft, Brian Brady, Dave Wright, Mike Nicholas, Barry Philbin. Substitutes: Billy Pickup, Bobby Wanbon.

First blood. Hooker Kevin Ashcroft reaches across the line for the first Warrington try at Wembley just after half-time. Alan Whittle had been tackled one yard short after a clever run and the ball ran loose. Dave Wright raises his arms to the skies.

Final flourish. Mike Nicholas scores the second Warrington try in the closing stages after beating four Featherstone defenders in magnificent style to seal a 24-9 victory. Warrington winger Mike Philbin is backing up while John Newlove, the Featherstone stand-off and captain, looks on helplessly.

Wembley winners. Warrington centre Derek Noonan, a self-employed plumber from St Helens, was famous for his strong defence but is pictured above making a break. Warrington full-back Derek Whitehead, a butcher by trade, kicked seven goals from all angles and distances to claim the Lance Todd Trophy as Man of the Match. Whitehead and scrum-half Gerry Helme are the only Warrington players to have won the award. Helme collected it twice, in 1950 and 1954.

Dropping in. Alex Murphy kicks one of his two drop goals during the final. It was his fourth Wembley win with his third different club after previous successes with St Helens (1961 and 1966) and Leigh (1971).

Well done. Prime Minister Harold Wilson leads the applause for Warrington's remarkable captain, coach and stand-off.

Running round Wembley with the cup. From left to right: Derek Whitehead, Dave Wright, Alex Murphy, Barry Philbin, Mike Philbin, Dave Chisnall, Alan Whittle. The Philbins were the first brothers to appear at Wembley.

Sweet dreams. Kevin Ashcroft catches up on his sleep on the coach home with wife Janet and four-year-old son Gary, the Warrington mascot.

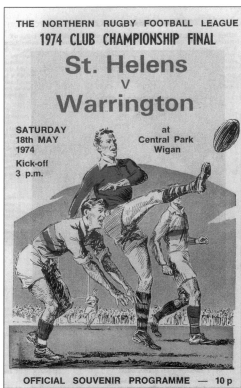

THE NORTHERN RUGBY FOOTBALL LEAGUE
1974 CLUB CHAMPIONSHIP FINAL

St. Helens
v
Warrington

SATURDAY
18th MAY
1974
Kick-off
3 p.m.

at
Central Park
Wigan

OFFICIAL SOUVENIR PROGRAMME — 10 p

Club champions. Almost 100,000 people turned out on the streets of Warrington to welcome home Murphy and his team, but Warrington had not finished collecting trophies. The Wire had already beaten Hull, Bradford Northern and Wakefield Trinity at Wilderspool to reach the final of the Club Championship against St Helens at Central Park. The final was played seven days after Wembley and attracted a crowd of 18,040 and millions of television viewers.

Pitch invasion. Alex Murphy is held high by supporters after the Club Championship final. It was a thrilling contest, played throughout in torrential rain, with Warrington deservedly winning 13-12. Winger Mike Philbin, prop Brian Brady, in his testimonial year, and centre Derek Noonan scored the Warrington tries with Whitehead kicking two goals. Whitehead's second goal took his total for the season to 162, equalling Harry Bath's club record set in the 1952/53 campaign. Loose-forward Barry Philbin collected the Harry Sunderland Trophy as Man of the Match. Philbin had been signed by Murphy from Swinton for £3,000 that February. Murphy described him as 'the final piece in the jigsaw' and how right he was. Philbin only played 16 games for Warrington that season and the Wire won the lot.

Grand slam. Murphy collects the Club Championship trophy, followed by Kevin Ashcroft and Derek Noonan, two of the ten men who had played in all four finals. The others were Derek Whitehead, Mike Philbin, John Bevan, Alan Whittle, Dave Chisnall, Brian Brady, Bobby Wanbon and Billy Pickup. In the left-hand corner is Phil Worthington, the Warrington secretary and director.

Beer delight. The Warrington changing room was a lively place to be after the Wire had collected their fourth trophy of an amazing season. Three Warrington players were selected for the Great Britain tour of Australia and New Zealand that summer – Ashcroft, Bevan and Nicholas. Unfortunately, Nicholas suffered knee ligament damage in the second half at Wembley and had to withdraw from the trip. Bevan capped a fine first season in Rugby League by becoming one of the stars of the tour. He played in four of the six Tests and scored 15 tries in 16 appearances (plus one as a substitute). Ashcroft, too, was an excellent tourist, making 13 full appearances and one as a substitute, but playing in only one Test.

Bevan salute. John Bevan soon became famous for his clenched fist salute with which he celebrated his many tries. During the 1974/75 season he touched down 29 times in 37 appearances, including this one against Second Division Batley at Wilderspool in the first round of the Player's No. 6 Trophy in September. Warrington won the game 36-3. Batley centre Phil Holmes, a former Leeds player, did not stand a chance.

Bull work. Brian Brady (above) was a massively strong player and the 54 tries he scored in 309 full appearances between 1965 and 1975 makes him the greatest try-scoring prop-forward in the club's history. In the days when all Rugby League players had full-time jobs, Brady worked as a welder. He also played five times for Lancashire and enjoyed a well-deserved testimonial season in 1973/74.

Mike Philbin joined Warrington from Swinton for £1,000 in March 1973 as a stand-off but was converted by Murphy into a right winger. He was one of the unsung heroes of the all-conquering 1973/74 season with 15 tries in 31 full appearances.

Running man. Second-row forward Tommy Martyn joined Warrington from Leigh in January 1975 and went on to play for Lancashire and England. He was another of Murphy's inspired signings, as proved by his career statistics of 51 tries in 219 full appearances for the Wire over the next six years.

The Warrington front row. Referee Gerry Kershaw makes his point to Dave Chisnall, Kevin Ashcroft and Brian Brady who, between them, made more than 600 appearances for Warrington in the days when winning the scrums was a vital part of the game.

Unsung heroes. Loose-forward Mike Peers carries the ball forward watched by full-back Norman Turley (in the background). One of the reasons for Warrington's successes in the early 1970s was the size and strength of the squad, so that players like Peers and Turley could step up from the 'A' team and cover for injured stars. Peers made 30 full appearances from 1974 to 1979 before moving on to Swinton, while Turley played in 26 games before joining Blackpool Borough. Turley went on to kick a record 97 one-point drop goals in his career.

Centre of excellence. John Bevan rated Frank Reynolds as the best centre he played with in Rugby League – praise indeed. Reynolds joined Warrington from Aberavon in August 1971 and, over the next four years, made 83 full appearances, scoring 16 tries, before injuries ended his career. Reynolds missed out on the Wembley win of 1974 but was in the beaten side against Widnes twelve months later.

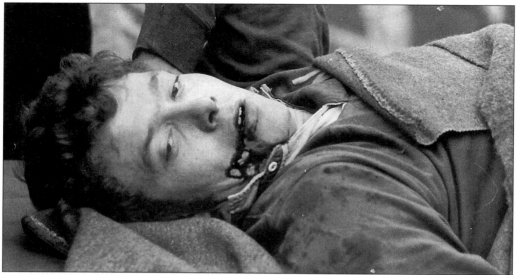

Where am I? Warrington centre Billy Pickup recovers from a high tackle suffered at Wigan in the third round of the Challenge Cup in March 1974. The game attracted a crowd of 21,178 and featured three sendings off – Colin Clarke, the Wigan captain and hooker, for the high tackle and Mike Nicholas and Wigan loose-forward Eddie Cunningham for fighting. Warrington won 10-6 thanks to three Kevin Ashcroft drop goals.

Same again. Warrington returned to Central Park in the second round of the Challenge Cup in February 1975. Again, three players were sent off (two from Wigan and Warrington's Bobby Wanbon) and again Warrington won in front of a 21,000-plus crowd. This time it was a more open game with the final score 24-17 and John Bevan (above) powering in for three of Warrington's six tries. Wigan full-back Bill Francis is the player giving chase.

Hat-trick hero. John Bevan leaves Alan Smith, the Leeds and Great Britain winger, trailing in his wake for one of his three tries against the Loiners in the 1975 Challenge Cup semi-final at Central Park which Warrington won 11-4.

Magic moment. Bevan celebrates the try in his own inimitable style. Leeds claimed that Bevan's second try that afternoon came from a move that began after the half-time hooter had sounded. Their objections were waved away; Warrington were going back to Wembley.

Royal welcome. Princess Alexandra chats to Warrington forwards Bobby Wanbon and Tommy Conroy before the start of the 1975 Challenge Cup final against Widnes. For Conroy, appearing in the final was a fitting reward for fourteen years of service to the club. He had made his Wire debut as a full-back in October 1961 when Brian Bevan and Jackie Edwards were still in the team and would make his final appearance in November 1975. In total, he made 262 full appearances (with another 50 as a substitute), scoring 27 tries. Conroy had signed for Warrington from Wigan Rugby Union Club and worked as a joiner.

Jumping for joy. John Bevan celebrates after putting Warrington ahead with a try in the fifth minute of the final. Widnes, however, went on to achieve a fully-deserved 14-7 victory. Alex Murphy later admitted, 'Things can go wrong. After all the *Titanic* sank, didn't it?'

Thank you. Four days after the final, Wilderspool was packed to see Warrington play England in the Alex Murphy testimonial match, marking his twenty years of outstanding service to the game. The testimonial fund raised a record £10,000 for the Warrington and England coach who is pictured in the changing room after the match. Murphy did not have much time to spend the money, however, because he was off to Australia, New Zealand and Papua New Guinea for six weeks with an England squad containing Chisnall, Gordon, Martyn and Noonan. Nicholas and Wanbon made the trip with the Wales squad. In July there were reports that Murphy had been offered £7,000 a year – a small fortune – to coach a Brisbane club, and three years at £6,000 each to take over at South Sydney. Murphy denied that any firm offer had been made, but it just showed how highly he was rated in Australia at the time.

End of an era. Murphy, now thirty-six, brought his brilliant playing career to a close by making one final appearance against Keighley at Wilderspool in September 1975. Fittingly, he finished on the winning side with Warrington scraping home 18-16. He is pictured above creating one of the two Wire tries for hooker Tony Waller. Second-row forward Peter Jewitt scored the other with Derek Whitehead kicking six goals. Murphy made just 66 full appearances for Warrington, laced with 9 tries, 12 goals, 28 drop goals and three sendings-off.

Alan Whittle scores one of the four Warrington tries against Wigan in the first round of the Lancashire Cup at Wilderspool in August 1975. Warrington, who had now entered a transitional phase, lost 39-14. Derek Finnigan is the nearest Wires' player to Whittle. Playing for Wigan, from the left, are Brian Hogan, Colin Clarke and George Fairbairn. Whittle joined Wigan that November.

Mr Angry. Dave Chisnall (above) is
restrained by Derek Whitehead and Gilly
Wright but still makes his point. Chisnall
moved on to Swinton in October 1975 with
Warrington receiving £5,000 and the less-
than-impressive Brian Butler in exchange.

Price is right. Joe Price missed the three
major finals of 1974 because he was serving a
four-month suspension but he returned to the
side to give more sterling service. In total,
Price made 128 full appearances for the Wire
during a twelve-year playing career stretching
from 18 September 1965 to 18 September
1977. His popularity on the terraces was
reflected in his testimonial season 1975/76,
which raised the impressive sum of £3,000

Match winner. Derek Whitehead lines up the successful touchline conversion that gave Warrington an 8-7 victory over Salford at Wilderspool in January 1976. Whitehead kicked 713 goals and 21 drop goals during his ten years with the Wire. He also scored 17 tries for a grand total of 1,516 points from 245 full appearances.

New blood. Former St Helens half-back Ken Kelly joined Warrington from Bradford Northern on loan in December 1976. At Wigan, in only his fourth match for the club, he suffered a broken arm but Warrington completed his £6,000 transfer while he was still injured. He went on to play for Lancashire, England and Great Britain, and win the Man of Steel award for the 1980/81 season.

Miller time. Warrington hooker and
captain Tony Miller holds aloft the
Locker Cup after the 27-15 pre-season
victory over Wigan at Wilderspool in
August 1976. Ian Potter (two), Tommy
Martyn (two), David Cunliffe, Derek
Finnigan and Dennis Curling scored the
Warrington tries

Knight time.
Stand-off Glenn
Knight kicked
three goals in
that win but
was better
known for his
try-scoring
exploits. He
grabbed 17
touchdowns in
just 37
appearances,
including four
at Barrow in a
Lancashire Cup
first round tie,
also in August
1976.

Rock on Tommy. Tommy Martyn touches down against Wakefield at Wilderspool in September 1976 with loose-forward Barry Philbin in support. However, Warrington went on to lose 31-15.

Handstand try. John Bevan performs more acrobatics, this time against Oldham at Wilderspool in April 1977. Warrington won 45-11 with centre Steve Hesford kicking nine goals.

No way through. Welsh winger Dennis Curling is stopped in his tracks by St Helens trio Roy Mathias (left), Eric Chisnall (centre) and Eddie Cunningham during the 1977 Premiership final at Station Road, Swinton. The game attracted a crowd of 11,178 on a sweltering May afternoon. St Helens were the clear favourites but Warrington were used to upsetting the odds and led 5-4 at half-time thanks to an Alan Gwilliam try and Steve Hesford conversion. The turning point of the match arrived early in the second half when Gwilliam and St Helens loose-forward Harry Pinner were sent off by referee Fred Lindop for fighting. The additional space created undoubtedly suited the St Helens style of play and they ran out comfortable 32-20 winners. The final turned out to be Curling's last competitive match for the Wire as he suffered a broken neck at Wigan in the Locker Cup match that August.

Bevans at the double. Dennis Curling was rightly awarded a testimonial season which raised the impressive sum of £3,500. The highlight of the fund-raising was a testimonial match that featured John Bevan and Brian Bevan on opposite sides.

One that got away. John Bevan is denied a try by Huyton player-coach Geoff Fletcher during a Lancashire Cup first round tie at Wilderspool in August 1977.

Loyal servant. Alan Gwilliam joined the Wire in January 1976 in the exchange deal that took Derek Noonan to St Helens. He went on to make 111 full appearances, scoring 18 tries. His most famous touchdown helped Warrington beat Australia 15-12 in October 1978.

Happy hooker. John Dalgreen joined Warrington from Halifax in September 1977 and was a key member of the team that won the John Player Trophy in January 1978. During the final, quick thinking by Dalgreen denied Widnes prop Glyn Shaw what would have been a vital try. Dalgreen later explained, 'I couldn't reach Shaw to tackle him so I just slid under him. He put the ball down on my legs!'

Youth and experience. Former St Helens captain Billy Benyon (left) and twenty-year-old prop forward Bob Eccles also played key roles during the successful John Player Trophy campaign of 1977/78. Benyon, thirty-two, and Frank Wilson, thirty-three, added much-needed experience in the centres while Eccles scored a cracking solo try in the 15-5 victory at Wakefield in the semi-final.

Mud larks. *Above:* Captain Parry Gordon and prop-forward Mike Nicholas after the 9-4 victory over Widnes in the 1978 John Player Trophy final. The game attracted a then record crowd of 10,258 to a rain-soaked and muddy Knowsley Road. Widnes were the clear favourites but coach Alex Murphy made sure that Warrington played the simple, no-frills rugby that the conditions demanded. Man of the Match Steve Hesford kicked three goals and set up the only try for John Bevan with a towering cross-field kick. The Warrington players collected a bumper £300 a man for their victory *Right:* The matchday programme.

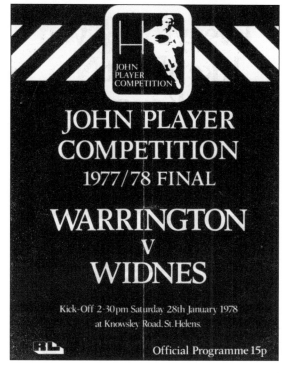

JOHN PLAYER COMPETITION

JOHN PLAYER COMPETITION 1977/78 FINAL

WARRINGTON V WIDNES

Kick-Off 2·30pm Saturday 28th January 1978
at Knowsley Road, St. Helens.

Official Programme 15p

Lion tamer. Tommy Martyn scores a try against Swinton (nicknamed the Lions) in a Lancashire Cup-tie at Wilderspool in August 1978. Loose-forward Mike Peers is backing up.

Golden boot. Steve Hesford kicked a club record 170 goals during the 1978/79 season. His total included 13 drop goals. Hesford also scored 5 tries for a remarkable haul of 342 points.

You beauty! A delighted player-coach Billy Benyon congratulates stand-in scrum-half Alan Gwilliam on the winning try against Australia on a memorable night at Wilderspool in October 1978. Warrington won 15-12 in front of a 10,000-plus crowd with Steve Hesford kicking six crucial goals. It was only Benyon's eleventh game as player-coach after taking over from Alex Murphy. The triumphant Warrington team was: Derek Finnigan, Mike Kelly, Steve Hesford, Billy Benyon, Joe Walsh, Ronnie Clark, Alan Gwilliam, Roy Lester, Tommy Cunningham, Mike Nicholas, Tommy Martyn, Brian Case, Ian Potter. The subs were Eddie Hunter and John Whittaker.

In the clear. Stand-off Ken Kelly heads for the try-line against Wakefield Trinity at Wilderspool in October 1978 to help the Wire on their way to a 19-13 victory. Kelly was Warrington's Player of the Year that season and was selected for the Great Britain tour of Australia and New Zealand but was forced to withdraw when he suffered a broken jaw in the last match of the season, a brutal Premiership semi-final against Bradford Northern at Wilderspool.

Coming through. Full-back Derek Finnigan steps through the Workington Town defence to score the only try in a 12-2 victory at Wilderspool in October 1978. Finnigan, who joined Warrington from Moore Rugby Union Club in 1973, made 230 full appearances for the Wire (plus 28 as a substitute), scoring 34 tries. He was famous for his superb last-ditch tackling and shrewd backing up.

Four star. One of John Bevan's best performances for Warrington came at St Helens in the opening league fixture of the 1979/80 season. Bevan was switched to loose-forward during the first half after Warrington had stand-off Ken Kelly sent off and lost prop Steve Hogan and No. 13 Mike Peers with injuries. Bevan, who had already scored a try from his usual position on the left wing, then tormented Saints with three more touchdowns as Warrington won 23-17. The match also marked an impressive debut by seventeen-year-old second-row forward John Fieldhouse, who came on as a first-half substitute. Bevan is pictured after touching down for his first try with an enthusiastic Eddie Hunter in support and St Helens backs Les Jones (left) and Derek Noonan looking on.

Get off! Games against Bradford Northern were often bad-tempered affairs. Here, referee Fred Lindop is in the process of sending off giant Bradford prop Ian Van Bellen during a typical encounter at Wilderspool in October 1979. Warrington went on to win 10-8 with John Bevan scoring the only Wire try. Three Bradford players were sent off that day along with Warrington's Tommy Martyn.

Young gun. Teenager John Fieldhouse was a fine example of Warrington's youth policy. Signed from the Wigan St Patrick's amateur club in June 1979, he had already played for Lancashire and England schoolboys and would go on to earn more representative honours in the professional game. While at Wilderspool, he played for Lancashire and Great Britain under-24s and made 92 full appearances for the Wire, scoring 16 tries. He was transferred to Widnes in January 1985 as part of the world record deal that took Andy Gregory to Warrington.

Vocal support. Powerful prop or second-row forward Roy Lester charges up field with encouragement from Ken Kelly (left) and with Billy Benyon in the background during one of his last games for the Wire. Lester made 82 full appearances for his home-town club after signing on a free transfer from Leigh in November 1976. He never gave less than 100 per cent and was an important member of the Warrington teams that won the John Player Trophy in January 1978 and achieved the famous victory over Australia that October. In July 1980 Lester became Fulham's first signing, even before they had persuaded Reg Bowden to become their first coach, but he returned to Wilderspool for a spell in charge of the Alliance team in November 1989.

Hard case. Alex Murphy signed Brian Case as a seventeen-year-old from the Blackbrook amateur club in St Helens in 1975 for just £300 and he repaid that modest outlay many times over during his seven years at Wilderspool. Case was an unspectacular but hugely-effective prop-forward who made 174 full appearances in primrose and blue before joining Wigan in January 1983 for a fee approaching £45,000. While at Wilderspool, Case played for Lancashire, England and Great Britain under-24s.

Getting better. Loose-forward Eddie Hunter was voted Warrington's most-improved player during the 1979/80 season and did even better the following year. He was a key figure as Warrington thrashed his home-town club Wigan 26-10 in the Lancashire Cup final in October 1980 and beat Barrow 12-5 in the John Player Trophy final in January 1981. Hunter went on to make 90 full appearances (plus 23 as a substitute) for the Wire, scoring 27 tries. He eventually moved on to Leigh at the start of the 1982/83 season in the deal which saw prop-forward Tony Cooke arrive at Wilderspool.

Two

The Australian
Invasion:
The 1980s

We've won the cup! Mike Gregory holds aloft the Lancashire Cup after the 24-16 victory over Oldham at Knowsley Road in October 1989. Gregory was one of Warrington's greatest loose-forwards. He captained his club and his country, making 222 full appearances for Warrington and winning 20 Great Britain caps.

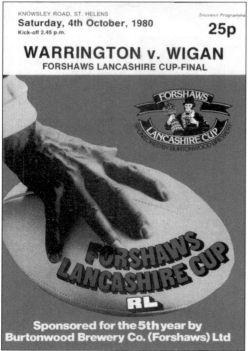

KNOWSLEY ROAD, ST. HELENS
Souvenir Programme
Saturday, 4th October, 1980
Kick-off 2.45 p.m.
25p

WARRINGTON v. WIGAN
FORSHAWS LANCASHIRE CUP-FINAL

FORSHAWS LANCASHIRE CUP
ESTABLISHED BY BURTONWOOD BREWERY

FORSHAWS LANCASHIRE CUP
RL

Sponsored for the 5th year by
Burtonwood Brewery Co. (Forshaws) Ltd

Bye George. Warrington second-row forward Tommy Martyn scoots past Wigan player-coach and full-back George Fairbairn on his way to a try in the third minute of the 1980 Lancashire Cup final. Warrington went on to beat their Second Division neighbours 26-10 with winger Steve Hesford claiming a record 17 points for a final from seven goals and a try. Unfortunately, the game, held at Knowsley Road, attracted just 6,279 supporters. The triumphant Warrington team was: Derek Finnigan; Rick Thackray, Ian Duane, John Bevan, Steve Hesford; Ken Kelly, Alan Gwilliam; Neil Courtney, Tony Waller, Brian Case, Tommy Martyn, Bob Eccles, Eddie Hunter. Substitutes: Tony Worrall, Ian Potter.

Top man. Warrington hooker Tony Waller holds up the trophy and the Man of the Match award after the 1980 Lancashire Cup win. Waller created tries for John Bevan and Rick Thackray as the Wire established a match-winning 17-2 lead after only eighteen minutes. A delighted Warrington chairman Brian Pitchford is in the right-hand corner of the picture. His wife Carol is on the left while another Warrington director, Ken Miller, is leading the applause behind the chairman. Ken Miller, of course, gave his name to the popular Miller Sevens competition for junior school children at Wilderspool.

Double trouble. John Bevan scored both the Warrington tries as the Wire beat Barrow 12-5 in the 1981 John Player Trophy final at Central Park. The first was created by Man of the Match Tommy Martyn and Ian Potter, the second was an interception effort from forty yards. Steve Hesford also kicked two goals and two drop goals in front of 12,820 fans, a (then) record for both the final and the tournament.

Party time. Warrington players and officials celebrate their third John Player success. From left to right: Brian Pitchford (chairman), John Whittaker (back), Neil Courtney, Ken Kelly, Mike Kelly, Ian Duane, Tony Barrow (back), Tommy Martyn, Jimmy Fairhurst (back), Tony Waller, Ian Potter. Warrington collected a cheque for £8,500 from the sponsors, taking their earnings in the ten years of the competition to a record £27,300.

JOHN PLAYER TROPHY

1980/81 FINAL
BARROW v
WARRINGTON

OFFICIAL PROGRAMME 40p

On the ball. Loose-forward Ian Potter was another top-class player that Warrington discovered but had to sell. Signed from the Blackbrook amateur club in St Helens in 1975, he made 115 full appearances for Warrington before signing for Leigh in September 1982 for £50,000, which was a record fee for a forward at the time. Hooker Tony Waller is the player in support.

High flier. Second-row forward Bob Eccles swoops for a try at Wigan in September 1981 during Warrington's impressive 22-11 victory. The referee is John Holdsworth from Leeds.

Try time. Warrington centre Ian Duane scores the winning try against St Helens at Wilderspool in October 1981. His delighted team-mates, from left to right, are: Brian Case, Ken Kelly, Mike Kelly, Derek Finnigan, John Fieldhouse. Duane, who was famous for his strong defence, made exactly 100 full appearances for the Wire from 1978 to 1985, scoring 15 tries.

Ouch! Welsh centre John Bevan connects with a high tackle during Warrington's 26-9 victory over Wigan at a misty Wilderspool on New Year's Day 1982. With Wigan still struggling to recapture former glories, the match was watched by just 3,669 fans. Ken Kelly (two), Neil Courtney and Phil Ford scored the Warrington tries with full-back Steve Hesford kicking seven goals. Wigan had prop-forward Glyn Shaw sent off after twenty-five minutes.

Man mountain. Neil Courtney was an old-fashioned and immensely powerful prop-forward who was Warrington's player of the season in 1981/82. Signed from St Helens in 1979, he made 131 full appearances for Warrington, scoring just 4 tries, including this one against Leeds at Wilderspool in January 1983. Courtney joined Wigan the following year.

Teenage rampage. *Above*: Nineteen-year-old stand-off Paul Cullen stretches for the line to score Warrington's try of the season against Barrow at Wilderspool in April 1982 after a magnificent run. John Bevan looks on proudly. *Right*: Eighteen-year-old loose-forward Mike Gregory makes a break with nineteen-year-old centre Ronnie Duane in the background.

Golden oldie. Veteran prop Dave Chisnall returned to Warrington for a second spell in October 1981 and again proved to be a great entertainer. Against Bradford Northern at Wilderspool in September 1982 he sold an outrageous dummy on the half-way line before setting off to the posts like a runaway train (left). He touched down at the Railway End and celebrated with a John Bevan-style salute (below).

Job well done. Warrington players and coach Kevin Ashcroft (right) reflect on their 16-0 Lancashire Cup final win over St Helens at Central Park in October 1982. At the front are captain Ken Kelly (left) and Man of the Match Steve Hesford. In the background, from left to right, are: Derek Finnigan, Paul Cullen, Paul Fellowes, Ronnie Duane, Mike Kelly.

Kelly's a hero. Ken Kelly is about to score the fourth and final Warrington try during the Lancashire Cup final triumph. Paul Fellowes, Mike Kelly and Bob Eccles had scored the first three with Hesford adding two goals.

Fast show. Spectacular tries were Rick Thackray's speciality and the exciting winger collected Warrington's Try of the Season award in 1983 for a typical effort against Oldham at Wilderspool that January. Bob Eccles (top left) started the move near his own line before passing brilliantly to Ronnie Duane (bottom right) with Thackray completing the job. Thackray scored 45 tries in 131 full appearances for Warrington during three spells with the club. Signed from Warrington Rugby Union Club in 1979, Thackray earned a Great Britain under-24s cap against New Zealand the following year.

Ball boys. Warrington players mark the opening of the new main stand in February 1983 by sending souvenir rugby balls into the crowd before the impressive 18-16 league defeat of Hull. The old wooden stand had burnt down in the space of twenty minutes one Thursday lunchtime in April the previous year. The cause of the £300,000 blaze was never discovered, although it was thought that a smouldering cigarette butt, innocently discarded at the previous evening's Warrington Amateur Rugby League Cup final, could well have started the fire.

Jumping for joy. Welsh winger Phil Ford celebrates a try against Hull in the Challenge Cup in March 1983, but that game would end in a controversial 10-4 defeat. Warrington were the better side but referee Billy Thompson disallowed four Wire tries.

Numbers game. Everything went right for second-row forward Bob Eccles during the 1982/83 season. He scored a remarkable 37 tries in 37 appearances to become the game's leading try scorer; he scored five tries in a John Player Trophy match against Blackpool Borough to equal the record for the competition and he won a Great Britain cap against Australia.

Money talks. Warrington captain Ken Kelly receives a Player of the Month award from chairman Brian Pitchford while, in the background, other players compare their pay slips – something they were strictly forbidden to do.

Light fantastic. Full-back Steve Hesford kicks a goal against Second Division Barrow during the 1983 Lancashire Cup semi-final at Wilderspool. Warrington, however, did not produce a sparkling display and lost 19-18. In the previous round at St Helens, Warrington had achieved one of the most remarkable victories in the club's long history. The Wire were leading 6-2 when tempers boiled over and Leigh referee Stan Wall sent off five players for fighting – Roy Haggerty and Steve Peters of St Helens and Phil Ford, Mal Yates and Mark Forster of Warrington. Bob Eccles and Mike Gregory were also sent to the sin-bin for ten minutes each, so that on two occasions Warrington were reduced to nine men. Yet, somehow, they still managed to win 30-26 in front of 5,047 disbelieving fans.

Eyes on the prize. Full-back Steve Hesford became the most prolific points scorer in the club's history, beating Brian Bevan's record of 2,288, when he kicked the second of his five goals against Huddersfield at Wilderspool in the first round of the Challenge Cup in February 1984. By the time Hesford was sold to Huddersfield in August 1986, he had extended his record to 2,416 points. His final total was made up of 1,112 goals and 47 drop goals (also both club records) and 46 tries from 310 full appearances.

Cup cracker. Mike Gregory touches down at the posts, with three would-be-tacklers left sprawling on the floor, for a magnificent try at Castleford in the second round of the Challenge Cup in February 1984. Hooker Roger O'Mahony is the Warrington player in support.

Centre of excellence. Former Woolston Rovers junior Ronnie Duane was the only Warrington player selected for the Great Britain tour of Australia and New Zealand in 1984. Tragically, after only eight minutes of the opening match against Northern Territory in Darwin he was carried off with torn knee ligaments and forced to return home. The injury did not end his career, but Duane, who was still only twenty, would never be quite the same powerhouse player again. Duane had earned the nickname 'Rhino' because of his strong running and would go on to make 158 full appearances for Warrington, scoring 51 tries.

Pass master. Former Widnes scrum-half Reg Bowden took over as Warrington player-coach in June 1984 after being in charge at Fulham for four years. Bowden (above, with Carl Webb in support) brought with him from Fulham a little-known Australian forward, Bob Jackson (left), and he would prove to be an inspired signing. Jackson was Warrington's Player of the Season in 1984/85 and would go on to make more than 200 appearances for the Wire. Bowden's next raid on his former club was not as successful. Full-back Steve Diamond, winger Hussein M'Barki and forward Dave Allen were signed as free agents in November in a controversial move. All three were no better than players already at Wilderspool.

Life savers. Seventeen-year-old scrum-half Paul Bishop swallowed his tongue after a hard, but fair tackle against Oldham at Wilderspool in November 1984. Bishop started having convulsions but physiotherapist Gordon Pinkney and coaches Derek Whitehead and Tony Barrow were quickly on the scene. They managed to release Bishop's tongue and save his life. Another scrum-half, Andy Gregory (right), joined Warrington from Widnes in a world record £75,000 deal on 21 January 1985 – twenty-four hours before the Challenge Cup deadline for signing players. Widnes received Warrington's transfer-listed forward John Fieldhouse and a substantial cash sum.

Turbo Ford. Welsh winger Phil Ford joined Warrington from Cardiff Rugby Union Club in January 1981 and proved an instant success, scoring on his debut against Featherstone. Over the next four years he collected 57 tries in just 110 full appearances before joining Wigan for £40,000, which was then a world record fee for a winger. Ford brightened many a Wilderspool afternoon with his dazzling running skills and his left-wing partnership with centre Ronnie Duane was a potent attacking weapon.

Flying Carbert. Winger Brian Carbert takes on Leeds in April 1985.

Power play. Carl Webb scores against Blackpool in September 1985.

Leading light. Phil Blake's record at Wilderspool speaks for itself. The Australian centre or stand-off ran in 41 tries in just 44 appearances for the Wire and was leading try scorer in each of his two seasons with the club (1985/86 and 1988/89). Unfortunately, each of his spells with Warrington finished in February because he had to return to his club in Australia ready for the start of their season. When it came to creating tries out of nothing, however, Blake had few equals.

Full throttle. Younger supporters may only remember Australian Brian Johnson as a deep-thinking and softly-spoken Warrington coach. In his playing days, however, he was one of the finest attacking full-backs ever to represent the club. In fact, his club record of 25 tries from the full-back position during the 1986/87 season may never be broken and is a lasting tribute to his pace and his ability to read a game. In total, Johnson scored 48 tries in exactly 100 full appearances for the Wire and some of them were truly spectacular efforts. In the 1985 Lancashire Cup final, in only his second game for the club, he scorched in from seventy yards against Wigan and in the 1986 Premiership final he carved his way through the entire Halifax team before sweeping in at the posts after coming on as a substitute.

Try star. Stand-off Paul Bishop scores against Halifax in the 1986 Premiership final, despite the attentions of Colin Whitfield, and with hooker Kevin Tamati and loose-forward Mike Gregory in close support. The final marked a dream come true for nineteen-year-old second-row forward Gary Sanderson (left) who had only made his Wire debut six weeks earlier after signing from the Thatto Heath amateur club in St Helens. Sanderson made eight appearances for Warrington before the end of the season and the Wire won the lot. He was twice capped by the Great Britain under-21s against France the following season. Sanderson's ability to punish opponents' mistakes by snapping up spilled passes earned him the nickname of 'The Hoover'.

Lap of honour. Delighted Warrington players show off the Premiership Trophy to the many Wire fans in the 13,000-plus crowd at Elland Road after the hugely-impressive 38-10 victory over champions Halifax. The scores had been tied at 10-10 at the interval before Warrington produced a magnificent second-half display. In the changing room after the match caretaker coach Tony Barrow was confirmed in the role. From left to right: Mark Forster, Paul Ford, Paul Cullen, Gary Sanderson, Mark Roberts, Mike Gregory.

Ford's Super Sunday. Warrington full-back Paul Ford was injured in the Premiership final against Halifax, but he had been outstanding in the earlier victories over Widnes at Wilderspool in the first round and at Wigan in the semi-finals. He is pictured here celebrating that famous 23-12 win at Central Park. Ford made 80 full appearances for the club between 1981 and 1987, scoring 5 tries and kicking 65 goals. He also kicked 7 drop goals.

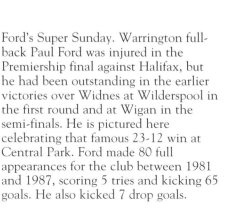

Crowning glory. Captain Les Boyd is carried by his team-mates after inspiring Warrington to that Premiership triumph with two of the seven tries. The *Manchester Evening News* reported, 'Boyd capped a great display by cutting inside for a try in injury time as well as charging over for the opening try in the second minute. Warrington's seven tries to one were the measure of their superiority over League Champions Halifax. They won because their pack overpowered Halifax in the second half and because their defence was so well organised.' Boyd had already become a folk hero at Wilderspool after signing for the Wire from Australian club Manly the previous June with

a bad-boy reputation. His signing was, therefore, quite a gamble but it paid off in spectacular style as he scored 13 tries in 33 appearances during the 1985/86 season. Boyd could break tackles, intimidate opposing packs and inspire those around him. Boyd, then aged twenty-nine, was not quite the player who had won 17 international caps for the Kangaroos but he was still a fearsome forward. Pictured here, from left to right, are: Billy McGinty, Paul Bishop, Paul Ford, Les Boyd, Paul Cullen, Gary Sanderson, Mark Forster, Mike Gregory, Bob Jackson, Mark Roberts. Ronnie Duane, Brian Carbert, Andy Gregory, Kevin Tamati and Brian Johnson are missing from the line-up.

On target. Paul Bishop scored 263 points for Warrington during the 1986/87 season. His impressive tally was made up of 12 tries, 99 goals and 17 drop goals.

Steamroller. Les Boyd continued to scatter would-be tacklers, as here against Castleford at Wilderspool in August 1986, until injuries disturbed his career.

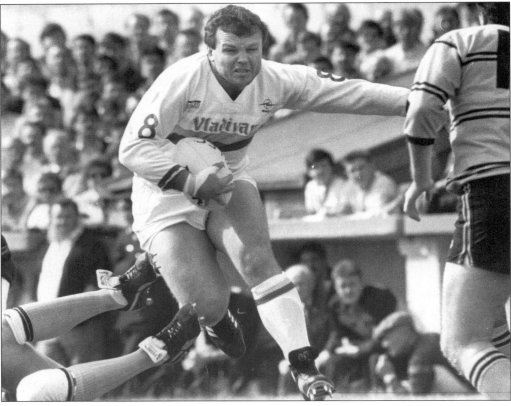

Making his mark. Second-row forward Mark Roberts was one of the stars of Warrington's 54-16 victory at Leeds in November 1986. Roberts scorched in for three of Warrington's twelve tries on an afternoon when the Wire, with scrum-half Andy Gregory running the show, looked unbeatable.

Simply the best. Many Warrington fans are convinced that Les Boyd, Kevin Tamati and Bob Jackson formed the greatest front row in the club's history. Between them they made more than 400 appearances for the Wire and never once took a backward step.

Killer Cullen. Centre Paul Cullen slides in for the try that gave Warrington a 6-4 victory at Wigan in front of a 17,000-plus crowd on New Year's Day 1987. Warrington had already beaten Wigan 23-12 at Wilderspool that October and so were completing a league double over the men from Central Park. Those two games were the only league defeats Wigan would suffer all season as they ran away with the title. Wigan, however, would take their revenge on Warrington by beating them in two major finals – the John Player Special Trophy final at Burnden Park, Bolton, in January and the Stones Bitter Premiership final at Old Trafford in May. The season saw Warrington generate record profits of £60,792, due mainly to the sale of scrum-half Andy Gregory to Wigan for a world record fee of £130,000 in January 1987. Rick Thackray (left) and Brian Johnson are the Warrington players in support.

In the corner.
Winger Mark
Forster scores
the only
Warrington try
in the 18-4
John Player
Special Trophy
final against
Wigan at
Bolton.

Dream debut.
Loose-forward
Mike Gregory
scores a try on
his Great
Britain debut
against France
at Headingley
in January
1987.

Joe Roe. Kiwi centre or second-row forward Joe Ropati powers over for Warrington's try of the season against Featherstone Rovers at Wilderspool in February 1987. Ropati scored 35 tries in 67 full appearances for the Wire.

Play on. Referee Fred Lindop throw up his arms as Cumbrian hooker Mark Roskell hands off former Warrington winger Phil Ford during a league match at Bradford in April 1987. Roskell had joined Warrington from the Millom amateur Rugby League club that March and went on to make 61 full appearances for the club.

Bulldog Drummond. Winger Des Drummond joined Warrington from Leigh for a club record cash sum of £40,000 in February 1987 and became a huge favourite at Wilderspool, scoring 69 tries in 182 full appearances. One of his tries (above) helped Warrington to an 18-8 victory at St Helens in the 1987 Premiership semi-final.

Turning point. Gary Sanderson heads for the try line during the 1987 Premiership final against Wigan. His score, however, was disallowed for an earlier infringement and Wigan went on to win 8-0. The final – the first to be staged at Old Trafford – attracted a record crowd of 38,756 who generated record receipts of £165,000.

Barrow boys. Warrington coach Tony Barrow (above) once again showed his skills in the transfer market with two key signings before the start of the 1987/88 season. John Woods (left) arrived from Bradford Northern for £40,000 in June while out-of-contract Widnes full-back David Lyon followed him to Wilderspool in August. In the latter case the clubs could not agree a fee and so, for the first time, Warrington had to visit the new Rugby League Tribunal, which valued Lyon at a bargain £12,500. Barrow even balanced the books by selling Alan Rathbone to Leeds for £32,000 and Bob Eccles to Springfield Borough for £25,000.

All change. Warrington forgot to take their kit to Castleford for the league game in September 1987 and had to borrow a reserve strip from the home team. But the change of colours did not seem to do them any harm as they won 40-30 with John Woods (above) collecting 24 points from 3 tries and 6 goals. Mark Roskell is the player in support.

Drummond special. Des Drummond left the entire St Helens team trailing in his wake at Wilderspool in September 1987 to score the Warrington Try of the Season.

Touchdown. Brian Johnson continued to be a regular try scorer with 10 in the 1987/88 season, including this one against Hull Kingston Rovers at Wilderspool in November.

Kiwi polish. New Zealander Kevin Tamati was a fine servant to Warrington. After signing from Widnes in August 1985, he made 105 full appearances for the Wire and was named captain for the 1987/88 season. He later coached the 'A' team and served as the town's Rugby League development officer for ten years. He has also coached Salford, Lancashire Lynx and Whitehaven. In the background are scrum-half Keith Holden (left) and centre Barry Peters.

Joker in the pack. Billy McGinty was one of the unsung heroes of the Warrington back-row in the late 1980s. After signing from the Widnes Tigers amateur club in June 1982 it took him three years to establish himself in the first team but he then went on to make 102 full appearances before moving to Wigan for £60,000 in August 1991. McGinty was the Man of the Match when Warrington won the Regal Trophy in 1991.

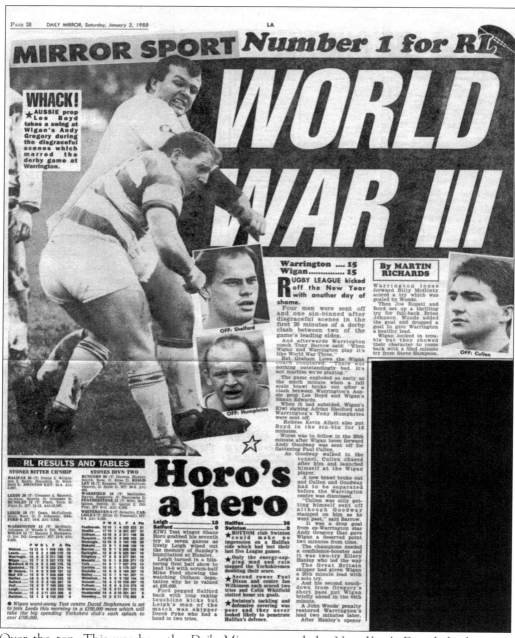

MIRROR SPORT Number 1 for RL

WORLD WAR III

WHACK!
★ AUSSIE prop Les Boyd takes a swing at Wigan's Andy Gregory during the disgraceful scenes which marred the derby game at Warrington.

OFF: Shelford

OFF: Humphries

OFF: Cullen

Warrington 15
Wigan 15

By MARTIN RICHARDS

RUGBY LEAGUE kicked off the New Year with another day of shame.

Four men were sent off and one sin-binned after disgraceful scenes in the first 20 minutes of a derby clash between two of the game's leading sides.

And afterwards Warrington coach Tony Barrow said: "When Wigan and Warrington play it's like World War Three."

But Graham Lowe the Wigan coach countered: "There was nothing outstandingly bad. It's not marbles we're playing."

The game exploded as early as the ninth minute when a full scale brawl broke out after a clash between Warrington's Aussie prop Les Boyd and Wigan's Shaun Edwards.

When it had subsided, Wigan's Kiwi signing Adrian Shelford and Warrington's Tony Humphries were sent off.

Referee Kevin Allatt also put Boyd in the sin-bin for 10 minutes.

Worse was to follow in the 20th minute after Wigan loose forward Andy Goodway was sent off for flattening Paul Cullen.

As Goodway walked to the tunnel, Cullen chased after him and launched himself at the Wigan player.

A new brawl broke out and Cullen and Goodway had to be separated before the Warrington centre was dismissed.

"Cullen was silly getting himself sent off although Goodway stamped on him as he went past," said Barrow.

It was a drop goal from ex-Warrington star Andy Gregory that gave Wigan a deserved point two minutes from time.

The champions needed a confidence-booster and it was two-try Ellery Hanley who led the way.

The Great Britain skipper had given Wigan a 20th minute lead with a solo try.

And his second touchdown from Gregory's short pass put Wigan briefly ahead in the 64th minute.

A John Woods' penalty restored Warrington's lead two minutes later.

After Hanley's opener

Warrington loose forward Billy McGinty scored a try which was goaled by Woods.

Then Joe Ropati and Boyd set up a thrilling try for full-back Brian Johnson. Woods added the goal and dropped a goal to give Warrington a healthy lead.

Wigan looked in trouble but they showed their character to come back with a 52nd minute try from Steve Hampson.

Horo's a hero

Leigh 18
Salford 0

KIWI Test winger Shane Horo grabbed his seventh try in seven games as lively Leigh wiped out the memory of Sunday's humiliation at Hunslet.

Leigh turned in a blistering first half show to lead 14-0 with scrum-half Mike Ford showing the watching Oldham deputation why he is valued at £90,000.

Ford pegged Salford back with long raking touchline kicks but Leigh's man of the match was skipper Derek Pyke who had a hand in two tries.

Halifax 36
Swinton 0

★ BOTTOM club Swinton could make no impression on a Halifax side which had lost their last five League games.

★ Only the energy-sapping mud and rain stopped the Yorkshiremen doubling their score.

★ Second rower Paul Dixon and centre Ian Wilkinson each scored two tries and Colin Whitfield slotted home six goals.

★ Swinton's tackling and defensive covering was poor and they never looked likely to penetrate Halifax's defence.

RL RESULTS AND TABLES

STONES BITTER CH'SHIP

HALIFAX 36 (T: Dixon 2, Wilkinson 2, Eadie, Meredith. G: Whitfield 6). SWINTON NIL: 24-0. Att: 4,987.

LEEDS 26 (T: Creasser 2, Basnett, Jackson, Morris. G: Creasser 6). HUNSLET 12 (T: Platt, Tait. G: Platt 2). HT: 14-6. Att:10,947.

LEIGH 18 (T: Dean, McCulloch, Horo, Kera. G: C. Johnson). SALFORD 0. HT: 14-0. Att: 2,818.

WARRINGTON 15 (T: McGinty, Johnson. G: Woods 2. DG: Woods). WIGAN 15 (T: Hanley 2, Hampson. G: tro. DG: Gregory). HT: 15-4. Att: 9,997.

	P	W	D	L	F	A	Pts
Widnes	13	12	0	1	348	130	24
Leeds	13	10	0	3	289	170	20
Warrington	13	8	2	3	311	185	18
Wigan	12	8	1	3	321	173	17
Bradford N	13	8	0	5	266	185	16
Castleford	13	7	0	6	233	274	14
St Helens	11	6	0	5	238	187	12
Hull KR	13	6	0	7	248	288	12
Halifax	14	5	0	9	265	260	10
Salford	13	5	0	8	182	261	10
Hull	12	5	0	7	169	253	10
Leigh	14	5	0	9	202	366	10
Hunslet	15	3	2	11	258	396	8
Swinton	13	1	2	9	142	350	4

● Wigan want-away Test centre David Stephenson is set to join Leeds this morning in a £100,000 move which will take the big spending Yorkshire club's cash splash to over £700,000.

STONES DIVN TWO

RUNCORN 20 (T: Davies, Hunter, Smith, Ross. G: Rose 2). KEIGHLEY 16 (T: Bragger, Winterbottom, Harris. G: Hirst 2). HT: 20-6. Att:656.

WAKEFIELD 16 (T: Mallinder, Rayne, Rapports. G: Harcombe 2). FEATHERSTONE 21 (T: Sibb, Bell, Quinn, Smith. G: Quinn 2. DG: Fox). HT: 6-11. Att: 4,356.

WHITEHAVEN 4 (T: Bolario. CARLISLE 0 (T: Mills. G: Tunstall). HT: 0-4. Att: 3,105.

	P	W	D	L	F	A	Pts
Featherstone	15	10	1	4	303	222	21
Sheffield	17	10	1	6	321	227	21
Oldham	13	10	0	3	311	146	20
Swinton...	13	10	0	3	245	155	19
Workington	13	10	0	3	152	135	20
Wakefield	15	9	1	5	308	271	19
Barrow	14	9	1	5	285	226	18
Springfield...	13	8	0	5	225	207	16
Keighley	17	6	0	9	277	301	16
Mansfield	15	7	0	8	336	271	13
York	14	6	0	7	327	273	13
Carlisle	15	6	1	8	179	227	13
Rochdale	13	6	0	6	164	267	12
Batley	15	5	1	9	197	207	11
Whitehaven	14	5	0	9	169	182	10
Doncaster	14	5	0	10	228	297	9
Fulham	14	4	0	5	215	275	10
Bramley	14	5	0	11	201	372	10
Huddersfld	14	4	0	10	201	301	8
Dewsbry	13	4	0	11	172	268	8

Over the top. This was how the *Daily Mirror* covered the New Year's Day derby between Warrington and Wigan at Wilderspool in 1988. Four players were sent off – Warrington's Tony Humphries and Paul Cullen and Wigan's Adrian Shelford and Andy Goodway – and Les Boyd was sent to the sin-bin. However, it was a compelling match watched by a near-capacity crowd of 10,056. Warrington and Wigan were each fined a record £3,000, £2,500 of which was suspended for a year, for the disturbances. The game itself ended in a 15-15 draw.

Points machine. Stand-off John Woods touches down at Widnes in the Premiership semi-final in May 1988. He also kicked three goals to take his points tally for the season to an amazing 351 in 37 matches.

Power play. Prop Neil Harmon developed into a fine forward during his seven years at Wilderspool. Signed from the Blackbrook amateur club in St Helens in January 1986, he went on to make 120 full appearances for Warrington before joining Leeds.

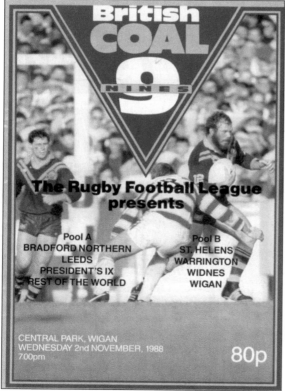

King Coal. Warrington players celebrate their success in the British Coal Nines competition at Central Park in November 1988. From left to right, back row: Billy McGinty, Brian Carbert, Gary Sanderson, Ronnie Duane, Robert Turner, David Lyon, Mark Forster. Front row: Mark Roberts, Mike Gregory (captain), John Woods, John Thursfield. Warrington beat Wigan 12-6 and St Helens 6-0 before defeating the Rest of the World 24-0 in the final. John Woods was voted the Player of the Tournament. Warrington's three short-term Australian signings that season – Phil Blake, Les Davidson and Steve Roach – were allowed to miss the tournament and go sight-seeing in Paris instead.

Coming to get you. Australian prop Steve Roach lines up Wigan winger Tony Iro during the 1989 Silk Cut Challenge Cup semi-final at Maine Road (above). The game attracted a crowd of 26,529 and was effectively settled by a record-breaking drop goal from Joe Lydon. The kick was officially measured after the match as being from sixty-one yards and inspired Wigan to a 13-6 victory. Three months later Warrington faced Wigan in an American challenge match in Milwaukee (right). Once again Wigan came out on top, this time 12-5, on a pitch that was too small to allow much flowing rugby to develop. The game marked the last appearance in a Warrington shirt by Les Boyd.

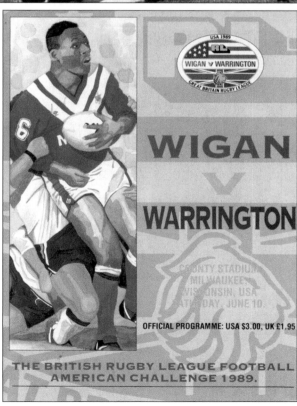

USA 1989
WIGAN v WARRINGTON
GREAT BRITAIN RUGBY LEAGUE

WIGAN
v
WARRINGTON

COUNTY STADIUM
MILWAUKEE
WISCONSIN, USA
SATURDAY, JUNE 10.

OFFICIAL PROGRAMME: USA $3.00, UK £1.95

THE BRITISH RUGBY LEAGUE FOOTBALL
AMERICAN CHALLENGE 1989.

Back to back. Warrington scrum-half Greg Mackey, on his debut, gets the better of Wigan's Andy Gregory on the opening day of the 1989/90 season. The match at Central Park ended with a 'Wigan Walk' (14,000 home supporters leaving early) as Warrington scored an impressive 18-6 win in the sunshine. This was Brian Johnson's (left) first full season in charge and exceeded all expectations. Warrington opened the campaign with six straight wins and were unbeaten in their opening ten matches. Johnson had replaced Les Boyd with a twenty-seven-year-old Yorkshireman, Tony Burke, signed from St Helens for a club record £50,000. Burke, who was 6ft tall and weighed 16st, added size and strength to the Warrington front row.

Double top. Warrington centre Tony Thorniley (right) scored two of the four tries in the 28-6 victory over Widnes in the Lancashire Cup semi-final at Wilderspool in October. Famously, he was wearing a pair of boots he had borrowed from injured second-row forward Mark Roberts. Australian second-row forward Bob Jackson (below) also scored two tries in the final against Second Division Oldham at Knowsley Road to seal a 24-16 victory and collect the Man of the Match award.

GRUNHALLE
LAGER
1989 R.L. LANCASHIRE CUP FINAL

OFFICIAL PROGRAMME
80p

OLDHAM v WARRINGTON
KNOWSLEY ROAD, ST HELENS
SATURDAY OCT. 14th ● KICK OFF 3.00pm

Lancashire lads. Warrington captain Mike Gregory holds aloft the Lancashire Cup with full-back David Lyon next in line. The victory celebrations had barely died down, however, when things started to go wrong. Greg Mackey's short-term contract expired and he moved on to Hull after receiving a better offer, while Bob Jackson had suffered a back injury that was to keep him out of action for three months.

Pitch party. From left to right, back row: Mark Roskell, Steve Molloy, Des Drummond, Robert Turner, David Lyon, Greg Mackey, Ronnie Duane, Mark Forster. Front row: Paul Darbyshire, Tony Burke, Mike Gregory, Tony Thorniley, Gary Sanderson.

Sing song. From left to right, back row: Mark Forster, Robert Turner, Mark Roskell, Tony Burke, Steve Molloy, Gary Sanderson. Front row: Paul Darbyshire, Greg Mackey, Tony Thorniley, Mike Gregory, David Lyon, Ronnie Duane.

Rocky. Robert 'Rocky' Turner took over the key stand-off role following John Woods' £50,000 move to Rochdale Hornets and excelled in the position, kicking 85 goals in 27 matches before a knee ligament injury ruled him out of the Challenge Cup final. Turner's progress was rewarded with a Great Britain under-21 cap against France and he was named Clubman of the Year by the Supporters' Club.

Lyon king. David Lyon developed into an exceptional player during his five years at Wilderspool. He cost just £12,500 from Widnes but was sold to St Helens for £90,000 – a (then) record fee for a full-back. He made 144 full appearances for Warrington, scoring 31 tries and kicking 112 goals and one drop goal for a tally of 349 points. He also played for Lancashire and joined the 1990 Great Britain tour of New Zealand as a replacement for the injured Alan Tait. However, success did not come easy: David worked hard on his attacking skills and also learned how to punt the ball huge distances upfield.

Three

The Dawn of
Super League
The 1990s

Regal Eagle. Des Drummond lifts the Regal Trophy after the 12-2 victory over Bradford Northern in the final at Headingley in January 1991. Drummond took over the captaincy from the injured Mike Gregory and was hugely popular with Warrington supporters. He was not quite so popular with journalists, however, because he refused to give interviews.

Wembley, here we come. Winger Des Drummond punches the air in delight after the 10-6 victory over Tony Barrow's brave Oldham side in the 1990 Challenge Cup semi-final at Central Park.

Try scorers. Mark Forster (left) and Martin Crompton scored the tries that took Warrington back to Wembley after a gap of fifteen years. Both players had latched onto inspired passes from 52nd minute substitute Mark Thomas.

Leading by example. Captain Mike Gregory scores at the posts during the 1990 Silk Cut Challenge Cup final against Wigan at Wembley. Gregory was easily Warrington's best player in a 36-14 defeat.

Consolation try. Full-back David Lyon scores Warrington's second try ten minutes from time. Mike Gregory had made a break from the base of a scrum before sending Lyon on a forty-yard run to the line.

Defeat hurts. Warrington players Bob Jackson and Des Drummond cannot hide their disappointment after the action is all over.

Welcome home. Wire captain Mike Gregory is lifted by the support of a large crowd at Warrington Town Hall the day after the final.

Thumbs up. Centre Chris Rudd (left) and stand-off Chris O'Sullivan celebrate the surprise 8-4 victory over Widnes in the Regal Trophy semi-final at Central Park in December 1990. Rudd scored the match-winning try and kicked two goals.

Official programme. Warrington rescued what was turning into a disappointing 1990/91 season with a brilliant run to lift the Regal Trophy for the fourth and final time. Using the £110,000 Leeds had paid for disgruntled prop-forward Steve Molloy in September, Warrington made a double swoop to sign Welsh Rugby Union internationals Allan Bateman and Rowland Phillips. Both agreed five-year contracts reported to be worth £100,000 and both played in the final against Bradford. The full Warrington team was: David Lyon, Des Drummond, Allan Bateman, Tony Thorniley, Mark Forster, Chris O'Sullivan, Kevin Ellis, Neil Harmon, Duane Mann, Gary Chambers, Gary Mercer, Billy McGinty, Paul Cullen. The subs were Mark Thomas and Rowland Phillips.

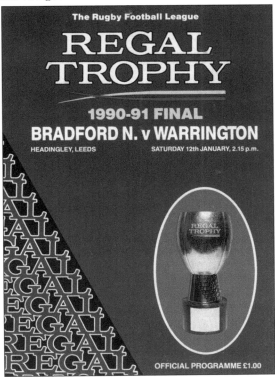

Super sub. Substitute Mark Thomas scores the only try of the match in the last minute of the Regal Trophy final.

Trophy time. Scrum-half Kevin Ellis (left) and centre Tony Thorniley go up to collect their winners' medals.

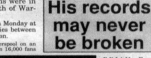

INSIDE THIS WEEK: EIGHT BIG PAGES OF WARRINGTON GUARDIAN SPORT

| Latest angling news, page 90. | Cricket special. See pages 90 and 91. | Darts and dominoes details on page 92. | Bowls round-up is on page 93. |

RUGBY LEAGUE LEGEND DIES IN SOUTHPORT AGED 66

Town mourns Brian Bevan

A GENERATION of Rugby League fans were in mourning this week following the death of Warrington winger Brian Bevan.

Bevan, who died in a Southport hospital on Monday at the age of 66, scored a world record 796 tries between 1946 and 1964 — including 740 for Warrington.

He played his last game for the 'Wire' at Wilderspool on an emotional Easter Monday in 1962 when more than 16,000 fans turned up to bid him farewell.

His funeral service is at Southport Crematorium, Southport Road, Scarisbrick, today, Friday, at 11.30am.

In the long history of Rugby League only two players have scored more than 500 tries — Bevan and Billy Boston.

His records may never be broken

Gentleman

Boston, who touched down 563 times for Wigan and Great Britain between 1953 and 1968, said this week: "Brian Bevan was the greatest I ever played against. He was a real gentleman.

"No-one will ever get near his record. He was unique. People talk about Martin Offiah but he isn't fit to lace Bevan's boots when it comes to try scoring."

Warrington RL Club President Clarrie Owen told the *Guardian*: "Words cannot really describe Brian Bevan. He was a one off. His try scoring was phenomenal.

"People used to say he couldn't tackle, but when he had to, against such as Wigan's Brian Nordgren or Huddersfield star Lionel Cooper, he pulled it off.

"I have been privileged to be born in an era which produced Brian Bevan."

FAREWELL...Brian Bevan waves goodbye to the Wilderspool crowd after his last game for the 'Wire' on Easter Monday, 1962. It was his 620th appearance for the first team and he scored off with his 740th try. Brian is with his wife, Doreen. More than 16,000 fans turned up to give him a rousing send off.

Brian Bevan's 'Wire' career

SEASON	GAMES	TRIES
1945-46	1	0
1946-47	42	48
1947-48	43	57
1948-49	44	56
1949-50	39	30
1950-51	40	60
1951-52	39	46
1952-53	41	66
1953-54	45	62
1954-55	37	61
1955-56	41	53
1956-57	26	14
1957-58	40	45
1958-59	40	54
1959-60	40	40
1960-61	42	35
1961-62	20	13
	620	740

Praise from MPs

MORE THAN 20 MPs have already signed a House of Commons motion praising Brian Bevan's contribution to Rugby League.

The motion, tabled by Warrington North MP Doug Hoyle, states: "This House very much regrets the death of Brian Bevan, a legendary figure in Rugby League.

"In the opinion of many he was the greatest winger to have graced the game and all of sport will be poorer for his passing."

THE *GUARDIAN*'S TRIBUTE TO BRIAN BEVAN CONTINUES ON PAGES 89, 94 AND 95.

By John Dickens

BRIAN Eyrl Bevan has left a world try-scoring record that will probably never be broken.

The Australian winger's scoring feats are detailed left and to those who were lucky enough to have seen him play, they will rekindle memories of brilliant scores.

For those who did not see him, they may find it difficult to believe such prolific scoring figures.

It was Warrington's good fortune when Leeds spurned the opportunity to sign him in 1945, although premature baldness and strapped up knees made him look the most unlikeliest of dazzling players.

Warrington gave him the opportunity, however, and he was to become a sensation in the next 16 years as he scorched through defences.

*continued on page 95.

TRY...Bevan heads for the line for yet another touchdown. In total, he scored 796 tries during his career.

THERE'S STILL NOBODY CHEAPER

COMPLETE EXHAUST SYSTEMS

TOP QUALITY LOWEST PRICES — FULLY FITTED

FROM ONLY £16.95

TYRES NEW STEEL RADIALS from £13.95 REMOULDS FROM £9.95

CLUTCHES FULLY FITTED from £49.50

BRAKES FRONT PADS FULLY FITTED from £9.99

NOW AVAILABLE CASH -'N'- CARRY
• EXHAUSTS • BRAKES UP TO 60% OFF R.R.P.
• SHOCK ABSORBERS • CLUTCHES

OPEN 6 DAYS A WEEK. Late night opening please ring for details. All prices include VAT

ALLEN STREET WARRINGTON   DEACON ROAD WIDNES

0925 232439   051-420 3858

OTHER BRANCHES ALSO AT

BUDJET

NOBODY BEATS BUDJET EXHAUSTS AND TYRES

CYCLE SALE

FREE DELIVERY

CYCLE SUPERSTORE
156 Cross St, Sale, Cheshire
TEL: 061 973 5688

LIFELINE WEEK 42
£1,000 WINNER
1496 D. Higham, Padgate

CASHLINE WEEK 54

Hold the back page. This was how the *Warrington Guardian* reported the death of Brian Bevan in June 1991. Bevan had scored a world record 740 tries in 620 apparances for the club during a remarkable career which stretched from November 1945 to April 1962.

Action Mann. New Zealand international hooker Duane Mann was one of the driving forces behind the Warrington team that reached Wembley in April 1990 and won the Regal Trophy in January 1991. He was also ever-present during the 1991/92 season, playing in all 32 of Warrington's games. In total, he made 121 full appearances for the Wire, scoring 20 tries, kicking 6 drop goals and serving as captain on a number of occasions.

Player of the Season. Kiwi Gary Mercer joined Warrington with Duane Mann in November 1989 and also made a huge impression at Wilderspool. Mercer began his Wire career in the centre but soon graduated to the second row where his appetite for hard work became an important feature. Mercer was Warrington's Player of the Year in the 1991/92 season, when he took his Wire statistics to 16 tries in 82 full appearances before joining Leeds.

Welsh wonder. Scrum-half Kevin Ellis, signed from Bridgend Rugby Union Club in May 1990, scores the match-winning try against Salford at Wilderspool on the opening day of the 1991/92 season.

Centre of excellence. Former Neath Rugby Union centre Allan Bateman was an excellent signing in September 1990. He went on to make 138 full appearances for the Wire, scoring 52 tries.

Work horse. Second-row forward Gary Sanderson was a key member of the Warrington pack for nine years, during which time he made 198 full appearances and 38 as a substitute. He also won four Great Britain under-21 caps (all against France) and was named Warrington's Player of the Season for the 1992/93 campaign. His service was rewarded with a testimonial season that raised the impressive sum of £31,000.

In full flight. Slightly-built winger Neil Kenyon scored a hat-trick of tries on his Wire debut against Barrow at Wilderspool in January 1990 and was Warrington's leading try scorer during the 1992/93 campaign with 13 in 22 matches. His overall return was an impressive 28 tries in 44 full appearances. Tragically, he took his own life in April 1997 when he was still only twenty-nine.

Young guns. Warrington's under-19s team do a lap of honour at Old Trafford in May 1993 after winning the Academy Cup in thrilling style by beating Hull 19-12 in the final.

Star in the making. Iestyn Harris was the star of the Academy Cup winning team and would mature into a world-class player, particularly after his £350,000 transfer to Leeds in April 1997.

Class act. New Zealand Test stand-off Kelly Shelford signed for Warrington in June 1991. He then received a better offer from Bradford Northern and signed for them as well. Once that minor problem was sorted out he went on to give excellent service during seven seasons at Wilderspool. He scored 44 tries himself and created many others with clever chip kicks. He was also at the heart of umpteen criss-cross moves involving centres Allan Bateman and Jonathan Davies.

Try of the Season 1994

"An incredible display of Welsh wizardry by Mr. Magic Jonathan Davies gave Wire a marvellous Challenge Cup fourth round victory at Halifax. The superstar conjured up two tries of world class. With the scores locked at 12-12, he touched down for his first super solo effort. After beating Paul Bishop, he raced 25 yards and flew past full back Steve Lay in the corner with inches to spare from the touchline." *WARRINGTON GUARDIAN*

JONATHAN DAVIES

Welsh wizard. Jonathan Davies added a new dimension to the Warrington attack and scored some memorable tries for the club.

Chambo. Prop-forward Gary Chambers was named Warrington's most improved player in 1993/94 after some barnstorming runs like this one against Sheffield Eagles.

Charge! Welsh forward Rowland
Phillips, pictured here with hooker
John Thursfield in support, was
more popular with Warrington fans
than he was with coach Brian
Johnson. As a result, he made just
27 full appearances for the first team
but was cheered long and loud each
time. In November 1994 Phillips
and Kevin Ellis were loaned out to
Workington Town for the rest of the
1994/95 season. Neither would play
for Warrington again. Ellis had
made 112 full appearances for
Warrington, scoring 35 tries. He
hads also won 10 caps for Wales and
toured with Great Britain in 1992.

Champions. Coached by Clive Griffiths (centre), Warrington won the Alliance Championship
for the first time in the 1993/94 season, finishing two points clear of Wigan and St Helens in
the final table. Iestyn Harris was outstanding at full-back, wing and stand-off for the 'A' team
and kicked 108 goals. His Great Britain Academy team-mate Mike Wainwright was equally
impressive at stand-off and loose-forward and was the sponsors' choice as Player of the Year.
The Warrington directors singled out hooker Colin Hodkinson who top-scored with 21 tries in
22 appearances. His playing career, unfortunately, would soon be ended by injury.

Eagle lands. Warrington attempted to build on the successes of the 1993/94 season by signing Great Britain under-21s stand-off Francis Maloney from Featherstone Rovers and rugged Australian forward Bruce McGuire (right) from Sheffield Eagles. McGuire certainly lived up to expectations with 7 tries in 37 appearances in the 1994/95 campaign.

The little general. Australian scrum-half Greg Mackey extended his club record of consecutive appearances to 98 in February 1995, but was beaten by a shoulder injury in his brave attempt to reach three figures.

Final letdown. Warrington saved their best displays of the 1994/95 season for the Regal Trophy, with victories over Doncaster, Salford, Keighley and Widnes earning them a place in the final. Warrington, as usual, were up against Wigan and were swept aside 40-10 in the first big match to be staged at the new £16 million Alfred McAlpine Stadium in Huddersfield. The match was all but over after twenty-four minutes, by which time Wigan had built up a 22-0 lead. Winger Mark Forster's two tries took his tally to six in major finals – a club record. The game attracted a capacity crowd of almost 20,000. Wigan centre Va'aiga Tuigamala is pictured getting the better of Rob Myler (left), Paul Cullen (rear) and Iestyn Harris. The Warrington team was: Jonathan Davies, Mark Forster, Allan Bateman, Iestyn Harris, Rob Myler, Francis Maloney, Greg Mackey (captain), Gary Tees, Tukere Barlow, Bruce McGuire, Paul Cullen, Paul Darbyshire, Kelly Shelford. The subs were Andy Bennett and Gary Sanderson.

Another super sub. Utility player Andy Bennett joined the action from the substitutes' bench 22 times during the 1994/95 season, a record for one campaign. His most telling intervention came against Halifax at Wilderspool. Warrington were trailing 4-0 when Bennett entered the fray after sixty-three minutes, but he scored two tries to help the Wire earn a 14-14 draw.

Best of enemies. In the original Super League plan in April 1995 Warrington and Widnes were merged to form Cheshire. Neither chairman, Jim Mills of Widnes (left) and Warrington's Peter Higham, would stand for that however and the plan was dropped.

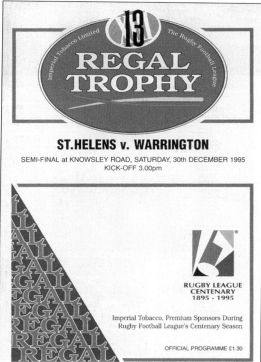

Fighting for his life. Cumbrian forward David Elliott broke his leg while playing for Warrington in an Alliance game in August 1995. Bone marrow got into his blood stream and he ended up on a life support machine. He pulled through but, at the age of twenty-four, would never play again. He stayed in the game, however, and went on to coach Woolston Rovers.

Record defeat. Warrington faced St Helens in a rearranged Regal Trophy semi-final at Knowsley Road on Thursday 3 January 1996. A close contest was expected. In the event, Warrington suffered a club record 80-0 defeat as St Helens ran in 14 tries and kicked 12 goals. The defeat was too much for coach Brian Johnson, a proud and intelligent man, who resigned after seven years in the post. He deserved a better fate.

Happy Lee. The Wilderspool floodlights shine on full-back Lee Penny after his hat-trick of tries against Leeds in November 1995. Warrington won 47-14 with stand-off Iestyn Harris contributing 23 points from 2 tries, 7 goals and a drop goal. Penny was Warrington's leading try scorer in the centenary season with 16 in 21 full appearances.

The Beast. A succession of arm and shoulder injuries has earned prop-forward Mark Hilton the tag of 'the unluckiest player in Super League', but when he is fit he is a formidable front rower. Including Super League IV, Hilton has made 83 full appearances for Warrington (as well as 33 as a substitute) and also represented the Great Britain Academy, Great Britain under-21s, England and Emerging England. Like Lee Penny, Hilton joined Warrington from Orrell St James, the amateur club that also produced Wigan and Great Britain captain Andy Farrell.

Dream team. Warrington North MP Doug Hoyle, now Lord Hoyle (centre), joins Warrington coach John Dorahy (left) and football executive Alex Murphy at the official opening of the short-lived Wolves Theme Shop in the Cockhedge Centre.

King Richard. Winger Richard Henare scored 29 tries in 31 full appearances during a brief and explosive career with the club.

Wolfie. Warrington ended 118 years of tradition before the start of the 1997 season by abandoning the nickname 'Wire' and becoming the Warrington Wolves. Many fans were furious and continued to chant 'Wire' from the terraces. However, the new club mascot 'Wolfie' became quite popular with younger supporters and, eventually, both nicknames were accepted.

Scully. Loose-forward Paul Sculthorpe was another triumph for Warrington's youth policy. First spotted by chief scout Jim Reader in 1992 playing for Oldham junior side Waterhead, he was signed as a seventeen-year-old two years later. He made his Wire debut in 1995 and won his first Great Britain cap in 1996. An impressive athlete, Sculthorpe also had wonderful ball skills and it was no surprise when he joined St Helens in a £370,000 deal – a world record for a forward – in December 1997. Sculthorpe had been one of the ball boys when Warrington played at Wembley in 1990.

French connection. Warrington played the ill-conceived Paris St Germain club four times during the first two seasons of Super League and won each encounter. This poster refers to the fourth and final game in August 1997 that Warrington won 17-10, thanks to two tries from Mark Forster, to end any fears of relegation. The match was played in the south of France and attracted a crowd of just 1,549 – nowhere near enough to support a professional club.

120

Overseas invasion. Warrington overdosed on overseas players during the 1997 season. From left to right, back row: Richard Henare, Salesi Finau, Nigel Vagana, Toa Kohe-Love, George Mann. Front row: Mateaki Mafi, Willie Swann, Kelly Shelford, Dallas Mead, Tony Tatupu.

Out of sight. New Zealander Nigel Vagana was a prolific try scorer at Wilderspool and his three touchdowns against Wigan on Easter Monday 1997 set up a memorable 35-24 victory. He finished the season as Super League's leading try scorer with 17 in 20 matches.

Danny boy. Australian prop-forward Danny Nutley is seen making his first appearance for Warrington in the pre-season friendly at Huddersfield in December 1997. His all-action style would make him Warrington's Player of the Year in Super League IV and earn him an extended contract. The Warrington player in the background is Adam Fogerty, who made just 4 appearances during the 1998 season before being released.

Eagar to please. Australian centre Michael Eagar leaves the Leeds defence trailing behind as he scores a sensational eighty-metre try at Headingley in April 1998. His effort was easily Warrington's Try of the Season. Ironically, Eagar went on to earn a reputation for excellent defensive play during his one season at Warrington before joining Castleford.

Love machine. New Zealand-born centre Toa Kohe-Love made a dramatic return from injury in 1999 to score 28 tries in 33 appearances and so become the game's leading try scorer. Ironically, Kohe-Love had been John Dorahy's first signing in February 1996 at the start of his unfortunate spell as Warrington coach. By the end of Super League IV, Kohe-Love had collected 46 tries for Warrington in just 77 full appearances with the hope of many more to follow. He is pictured sprinting through a huge gap in the Hull Sharks defence at Wilderspool in August 1999.

Can you kick it? Scrum-half Lee Briers was Darryl Van de Velde's first signing as Warrington coach and cost a reported £65,000 from St Helens in April 1997. Briers became a master of the 40-20 kick and a useful place kicker. By the end of 1999 he had kicked 177 goals and 17 drop goals for the Wolves and stood to benefit enormously from the signing of Australian half-back legend Allan 'Alfie' Langer for Super League V.

All smiles. Winger Jason Roach (left) and prop Mark Hilton share a joke after the impressive 34-4 televised victory over Halifax at Wilderspool in the Silk Cut Challenge Cup in February 1999. Roach had made history on his Wolves debut at Wakefield the previous year by scoring four tries.

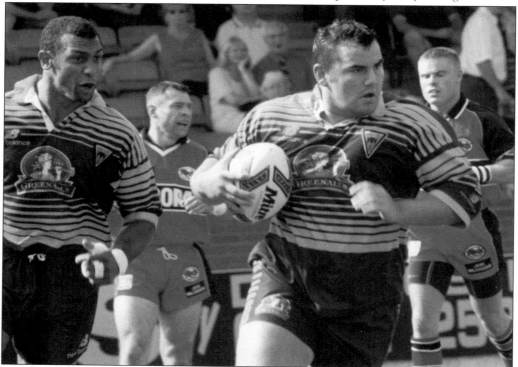

Man mountain. Giant second-row forward Steve McCurrie was Warrington's Player of the Season in 1998 but struggled with injuries in the following campaign. Here he scores a try at Salford in September 1999, with vocal support from former Great Britain centre Alan Hunte.

Hand off.
Warrington centre
Jon Roper hands
off a Castleford
player with Alan
Hunte again in
support. Roper's
obvious talents had
earned him a place
on the ill-fated
Great Britain tour
of Papua New
Guinea, Fiji and
New Zealand in
1996.

Stalwart. Mark
Forster was still
going strong in
1999: his
eighteenth season
in the first team.
By the end of the
year he had scored
186 tries in 428 full
appearances.

Penrith Panther. Australian hooker Danny Farrar was Warrington's major signing for the 1998 season and captained the Wolves throughout a difficult campaign. Signed from the Penrith Panthers club, Farrar even turned out at scrum-half later in the season to help his new team. He started the 2000 season in top form with two tries at Hunslet as Warrington recorded an impressive 46-4 victory in the fourth round of the Silk Cut Challenge Cup.

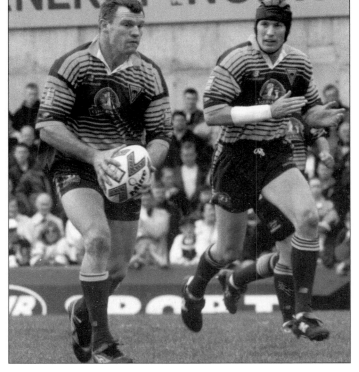

Bulldog spirit. Australian second-row forward Simon Gillies joined Warrington from Canterbury Bulldogs for the 1999 season and took over the captaincy from Danny Farrar in May. Gillies, pictured here with loose-forward Mike Wainwright in support, scored 6 tries in 31 appearances during his one season with the club.

Try hunter. Former St Helens centre Alan Hunte scored 21 tries in 32 appearances during his first season with Warrington. Included in his total were hat-tricks against Featherstone Rovers in the cup (above) and at Huddersfield in the league (right).

Dinner time. Warington coach Darryl Van de Velde hands out the awards at the annual presentation dinner in October 1999. Prop Danny Nutley was the Coach's Player of the Year, centre Toa Kohe-Love was the Players' Player of the Year and second-row forward Ian Knott was the Most Improved Player.

Welcome to Wilderspool. Darryl Van de Velde welcomes new signings, scrum-half Allan Langer (left) and prop-forward Andrew Gee. Both had enjoyed enormous success with Brisbane Broncos and captained the team. Langer had been voted Australia's Player of the Decade for the 1990s, while Gee was the type of big forward that Warrington had been missing for several seasons. They are expected to make a massive impact.